⟫⟩52⟨⟪
WAYS TO
EVALUATE
YOUR
CHILDCARE
OPTIONS
... and gain peace of mind

52

WAYS TO

EVALUATE

YOUR

CHILDCARE

OPTIONS

. . . and gain peace of mind

Jan Dargatz

OLIVER
NELSON

THOMAS NELSON PUBLISHERS
Nashville • Atlanta • London • Vancouver

Published in Nashville, Tennessee, by Thomas Nelson, Inc., Publishers, and distributed in Canada by Word Communications, Ltd., Richmond, British Columbia.

Library of Congress Cataloging-in-Publication Data

Dargatz, Jan Lynette.
    52 ways to evaluate your childcare options / Jan Dargatz.
        p.   cm.
    ISBN 0-8407-9263-8 (pbk.)
    1. Day care centers—Evaluation.   2. Child care.   I. Title.
II. Title: Fifty-two ways to evaluate your childcare options.
HV851.D27   1994
362.7'—dc20
                                                                94-6140
                                                                CIP

Printed in the United States of America.

            1   2   3   4   5   6 — 99   98   97   96   95   94

To
My friend
Dr. Cherie Dawson-Williams
for the example of her life and work
in providing quality, loving day care for children

✦ Contents

✦ Introduction
"A Precious Trust"

Children are precious beyond measure. That fact cannot be overemphasized or overstated. The vast majority of parents regard their children as the top priority in their lives, and they spend most of their energy, concern, and time attempting to secure and implement a healthful, nurturing, loving environment for their children.

The parental desires to protect and provide are challenged by the idea of childcare facilities or day-care providers. If given the choice, many mothers and quite a few fathers would rather stay at home with their children than work away from them all day long. The facts are, however, that

- many parents don't have a choice. Single parents must leave their children in the care of others to be able to work and provide the basics of life. Low-income two-parent families face this same challenge.
- many parents don't feel they have a choice. These parents tend to regard their parental role as lying beyond the provision of basics to include provision of enrichment and opportunity. The money earned from a career

(or two careers) is necessary, in their opinion, to pay for family goals related to travel, toys, camps, lessons, and certain possessions regarded as helpful to their child's growth and development. For these parents, day care may be a means to an end or, in the case of early learning centers, a part of the end goal.

- other parents don't want to have to make a choice. These parents tend to hold to the opinion that a happy, fulfilled parent produces a happier, more fulfilled child. For them, day care is a part of the way in which both parental and child needs can be met in balance.

This book does not attempt in any way to convince you that you should or should not pursue day care. Rather, the assumption is made that you have already made a choice to secure day care for your child, and that you want to provide the best possible alternative to your all-day-at-home presence.

The key premise behind all of the suggestions in this book is this: *to the best of your ability, provide what is best for your child.*

Keep your child—and very specifically, your child's needs, abilities, and personality—at the forefront of your decision making. Don't choose a childcare option on the basis of cost, availability, accessibility, or school philosophy alone.

Start with your child. How does she respond to particular environments? Where can he best experience a family-away-from-the-family atmosphere? How much supervision or one-on-one contact does she need? In what areas does he need to mature or grow?

No single day-care provider can meet all of your child's needs, but you can ensure that you have chosen the provider with the greatest potential for meeting as many of your child's needs as possible.

Do you like what you see, what you feel, and what you hear? Are you totally at ease in the environment? Are you confident that the day-care center will deal with your child as if your child is your most precious treasure—and, indeed, the center's most precious treasure, too?

When you are confident that the childcare option you have selected is the right one for your child, you will have a strong sense of assurance and an eager anticipation that your child is about to experience something good and beneficial to growth. If you don't have that confidence, make another choice.

Day care can truly be a plus in your child's life. Do your utmost to make it so.

1 ✳ An Overview of Options

Most parents have at least ten options when it comes to providing day care for their children.

1. In-Home Care This person may be a part-time baby-sitter, a full-time helper (who may have other chores besides childcare), or a live-in nanny.

2. Other-Family Day Care The day-care provider is usually a mother with children of her own who takes additional children into her home —usually providing something of a neighbor-to-neighbor service. In some cases, the "other mother" may be a relative to the child. Most states require licensing, or registration, for these homes (based upon the number of children receiving care, including the mother's own children). However, most mothers who provide this service aren't licensed.

3. Family-Day-Care-Agency Homes These homes are supervised by a local family day-care agency, and usually, the person needing day care is matched to a provider so that the child experiences the greatest amount of similarity between home and the day-care home. The persons who provide this care attend childcare workshops and receive ongoing supervision.

4. Nursery Schools and Day-Care Centers These vary widely. The common threads tying these centers together are

- identifiable facilities that tend not to be used for any other purpose—such as a renovated house; a portion of a campus, office building, factory, or church; or a freestanding building.
- full-time staff. Even though the center may be open only half a day, some staff members are usually employed full-time to administer the program or provide care.
- set hours of operation.
- outside regulation. These centers are nearly always under the regulation of a state agency.

5. Early Learning Centers These preschools or day-care facilities emphasize training children according to developmental level. The programs tend to be highly structured.

6. Infant Care Centers These may be a part of nursery, day-care, or early learning centers, or they may be stand-alone facilities. Licensed infant care providers usually must have a ratio of one

provider to no more than four babies, and more commonly one adult per two children.

7. After-School Care   These centers usually operate only during after-school hours, and they bridge the gap between the time school is out and the time a parent can pick up the child. Some centers are open twenty-four hours a day (providing a service to parents who must work night or evening shifts). These programs generally have vacation and summer hours.

8. Sick-Child Care   Most day-care facilities request that parents keep sick children at home, which creates a problem for parents who must work. Sick-child facilities fill the gap.

9. Play Centers   These are usually drop-off centers where a parent can leave a child for just a few hours, usually while the parent shops, attends a meeting or event, or has some parent-alone time.

10. In-Work Child Centers   These centers are usually "engineered" by employees within their own work environment. For example, a group of parents might request permission to hire a childcare provider to take care of their children in an empty office down the hall. The company, of course, assumes liability for children on its premises. The parents assume the cost or negotiate the care as part of a benefits package.

2 ✴ First Questions

Your search for a childcare provider is likely to begin with a series of phone calls.

Sources Begin by calling relatives and friends who have had successful day-care experiences. You may also want to call your pediatrician.

The personnel office of your company may have a list of recommended day-care providers. Religious organizations and churches frequently have day-care facilities. If your specific church or synagogue doesn't offer day care, you might ask your minister or rabbi to suggest a synagogue or church within your denomination that does.

Children and family service agencies, such as the YMCA, sometimes have lists of recommended day care. City and state agencies can also provide recommendations.

You'll probably want to make several calls and look for a convergence of positive opinions.

Calling the Centers When you call the centers, you'll want to get answers to these preliminary questions:

- "What hours of care do you offer?"
- "What days of the week do you offer care?"
- "What ages do you serve?"
- "Do you have an opening for my child's age?" (If not, what is the waiting period?)
- "Are you licensed?"
- "Do you provide transportation?"
- "How large are your classes (or groups)?"
- "Do you serve meals?"
- "Where are you located?"
- "What are your fees?"
- "Do you have a particular learning philosophy or approach?" (For example, is it a Montessori school, or does it offer a special curriculum?)
- "Are your teachers degreed and experienced?"

You might also ask if the center or person has some parent names that you might call for reference.

3 ✳ The Center's Educational Philosophy

Educators recognize three basic philosophies toward the training and development of young children. Even if you are hiring a full-time baby-sitter, you'll want to find out which of these philosophies is at work.

Child-Directed In this approach, children set their own schedules and follow their own instincts. Play is quite freewheeling, with very little interaction with adults. Play is considered the primary means of exploring the world and is regarded as the most educational activity in which a child can engage prior to formal schooling.

Many young children thrive in this atmosphere. They develop their own identity, sense of priority, and play relationships easily and naturally. Other children need more structure and involvement with adults.

Teacher-Directed In these environments, all activities are planned and supervised by teachers. Adults frequently lead discussions or guide games. Supervised arts and crafts are often a major part of the day's activities.

Some children love structure and are eager to learn along prescribed lines. They usually have plenty of play opportunities at home with family members and neighborhood friends. Other children feel stifled.

Learn-and-Play Linkages In between teacher-directed and child-directed facilities are centers in which learning and playing are meshed together. For example, the Montessori approach might be considered a child-directed approach to learning rather than a child-directed play approach. Teachers and adults become part of the learning resources made available to each child.

Other centers mix play and learning in projects—for example, working on plays (from writing scripts to designing costumes to performing), singing together, planting seeds together to grow a group garden (and later weeding, watering, and harvesting together). The activities are not explained or taught as much as they are done, usually in a way the child enjoys and counts as play.

Teachers who take this approach tend to listen more than talk and to guide a child's desire to explore. In many cases, children play and talk freely, and the teacher picks up their interests and guides them toward an activity, game, or discussion. This environment is by far the most difficult for a teacher since it requires great sensitivity and day-by-day flexibility. Most children, however, seem to flourish when this approach is taken and it is skillfully implemented.

Ask and Watch   Ask a center director, baby-sitter, or teacher about the approach. Listen closely to examples she provides or reasons she gives for what she does with the children under her supervision. And then watch her in action with a group of children. Does the teacher actually do what she claims is her philosophy?

4 ✳ Licensing and Accreditation

One of the first questions most parents ask a child-care provider is this: "Are you licensed?"

The other-family day-care provider is probably *not* licensed or even registered with a state agency. That is not to say, however, that the person is not qualified or even the best person to provide care for your child. Chances are, the hours are more flexible, the care more personal, and the home more familiar than many other choices at your disposal. If you opt for this type of childcare, you'll probably want to know the names of the other parents who are leaving their children with this provider so that collectively, you might exchange information or concerns. In essence, you'll be forming your own regulatory group.

Licensing Consider what it means for a facility to be licensed. Licensing is by either city or state. Usually, the agency has something to do with institutions or social services. A licensed center or home is usually required to keep its license permanently on display.

Different standards   Nearly all states evaluate the physical safety and cleanliness of a facility—including the safety of playground (or yard) areas and play equipment. Centers must conform to all fire safety and health department codes.

Another area considered in the licensing process is the ratio of staff to children. That ratio usually varies by age, for example, one teacher for every five children ages two to three, with no group larger than ten children. The ratio is not fixed from state to state. In fact, no rules regarding the licensing of day care are uniform nationwide. To know what a day-care license means, you need to know what the regulations are for licensing a center in your city or state.

Licensing standards also usually cover disciplinary measures. Generally speaking, corporal punishment (including spanking, slapping, or rapping knuckles), the use of abusive language (including profanity), humiliation of children (including shaming or "scare" tactics), and the use of any type of punishment associated with eating, rest, or toilet training are prohibited.

Regulatory visits   The advantage of licensing is twofold. The facility must meet certain basic standards initially, subject to verification by an on-site visit. And the facility is inspected periodically to make certain that the initial standards are being maintained.

Registration   A form of regulation being tried in some states is that of registering day-care providers. It is a voluntary process and does not require visits to the site. The caregiver places on file a set of forms and papers describing the facility and qualifications. This has an advantage in helping a caregiver focus on what is considered important by the state. The state, however, does not confirm the truthfulness of an applicant's statements. Note that registration is *not* licensing.

Accreditation   Accreditation refers to approval given to a day-care center by a group of educators. This is a fairly recent phenomenon among preschools, but an increasing number of centers are seeking accreditation. Educator review committees require that centers have a clear statement of purpose and that they implement that purpose to a high degree of quality. Fully accredited facilities are usually quick to say so.

5 ✳ The Caregiver's Credentials

Ask very directly about the people caring for your child and why they are qualified to do so.

Qualifications If you are hiring an individual (in-home or other-family care), you will want to conduct a thorough background check. How long has the person lived in your present community? For what families has the person provided care?

Speak to the director of a facility you are considering. The director of a preschool should be trained in early childhood education (preferably with a master's degree) and have at least two years' experience teaching young children. Ask, too, about the credentials of the teachers or caregivers. Teachers should have professional early childhood training or comparable experience.

Ask specific questions about the teaching assistants. Are they mature—nineteen or older? Do they have at least a high-school education and some training in childcare?

Ask how the teachers and aides are recruited, and how long the average teacher or assistant stays at the center. A high turnover rate can create instability for your child.

Staff Interaction   When you visit a day-care facility, note the way the director interacts with the staff and students. Does the director

- show respect for teachers, assistants, and children?
- provide positive guidance?
- listen intently to children or staff members?
- address others in a kind, straightforward manner?

As you talk with the center's director, you should feel assurance that the person is answering your questions fully, professionally, and candidly. Ask about the personal philosophy of education and the goals for the children who attend the facility. What matters most about the children under the director's care? Listen closely to the answer. The director who says, "That each child is happy," operates the program in a quite different manner from the director who says, "That each child is prepared to enter kindergarten with appropriate learning and socialization skills."

CDA Credentials   The Child Development Associate (CDA) credential program provides two tracks for credentialing day-care workers: one is an experience track, and the other is a means of formal training in child development and a follow-up evaluation of a person's competency in working with children.

6 ✳ Safety Issues

The outer appearance of a childcare facility should not be your primary concern. Rather, you should focus on issues of safety, security, and the creation of an age-appropriate environment.

Lead Paint and Asbestos If the facility is housed in an old building—either residential or commercial—ask specifically about the presence of lead paint and asbestos. Permanent brain damage can result from lead poisoning, and major lung disease and cancer have been linked to breathing tiny asbestos particles. Young children, of course, are apt to suck or chew on anything within their reach, including painted wood surfaces. It is not enough that the surface has been painted over. Rather, every bit of the lead paint should have been scraped away. (Most buildings built before 1970 were painted with lead-based paint.) Ask about painted furniture, too.

Structural Safety Look for rotting wood, falling plaster, shaky stair rails, or wet spots in the yard that may indicate a backed-up septic tank. Are electrical outlets plugged with safety plugs? Are electrical wires within reach of young children? Are cabinet doors latched with childproof latches?

Windows New-building construction codes in most states currently call for at least 10 percent of the total wall space in a room to be glass. Are the windows low enough for your child to reach in case an escape is necessary? Are the windows screened or secured in some way so that children cannot accidentally fall out of them? Are the window coverings securely attached—preferably shutters rather than long drapes? Is there safety glass in glass doors and windows?

Furniture and Equipment Check Look
for these musts:

- All fans should be out of a child's reach.
- All heavy furniture and room dividers should be firmly anchored.
- Table corners should be rounded.
- Bookshelves should be low and limited to one or two shelves in height (so that children can't climb them or cause them to topple over).
- The environment should have very few breakables.
- No swallowable items should be within a child's reach.
- Outdoor play equipment should be geared to the age of the children in the center (with

play areas divided according to age if the
center has a wide range of ages).
- Toys, cribs, and other furniture used by the
  children should be in good repair.
- Floors should be free of floor rugs or pro-
  truding electrical outlets.
- Children should be able to open doors from
  the inside out, such as crash-bar doors that
  may be locked to the outside world but
  opened from the inside in case of an emergency.

7 ✦ Health Issues

Licensed day-care centers are required to check all children on a daily basis for illness. They are required by law to have a sick child seen by a health-care professional (usually a nurse). Nevertheless you have no guarantee that your child won't come home with pinworms, lice, chicken pox, or the flu.

Ask a day-care administrator these basic health-related questions:

- "What is your sick-child policy?"
- "Do you have an isolation room in which sick children are kept?"
- "How is the facility kept clean? How often are floors mopped and hard surfaces cleaned with a bleach-based disinfectant? How often are toys cleaned, and in what manner?"

Fresh Air Ventilation is frequently a problem in older buildings. If you sense that the air in a facility is stale or that there seems to be a pervasive odor, ask when the vents and air ducts were last cleaned. Ask, too, how often the children engage in outdoor activities.

Soap and Water Every preschool should have the following:

- Running water and plenty of soap, readily available for hand washing by children and teachers
- Paper towels
- A first aid kit (for treating minor cuts, scrapes, and abrasions)

Children and all staff members should wash their hands when they arrive at school, before eating any food, after toileting, and after contact with any body fluids (wiping a child's nose, cleaning a skinned knee, wiping away tears, and so forth).

Rest Room Facilities Perhaps the most important architectural feature related to a child's health in a day-care setting is the rest room. Sinks and toilets should be low so that a child can use them without adult assistance. If you are taking your child to a home setting, ask which bathroom the children use and whether they use it exclusively. If the bathroom is used by other members of the family, ask if their personal items are stored securely (such as curling irons, razors, toothbrushes).

AIDS To date, no reported case of AIDS has been linked to transmission in a childcare setting. Still, 2 percent of AIDS cases have been children (most contracting HIV from their mothers during pregnancy). The disease is not spread by skin contact with urine, stool, vomit, saliva, or tears. It cannot be contracted by playing with a toy, hugging, or wiping a nose. The most serious possibility for transmission could be an infected child with an open sore in the mouth biting another child (to the point of bleeding).

8 ✳ Security Issues

Parents must register concern about the security of any facility in which they wish to leave their child—even if it's for only an hour or two.

Standard Security Measures Ask about the security measures. Some of them will be obvious, such as fences around play areas and locked outside doors. Ask about the check-in and check-out procedures required of adults (from delivery persons to parents) who might come and go from the center. Ask about procedures to ensure that your child is not released to an adult other than you or your spouse or other designated adults at any time.

Some centers will release a child only to persons on a designated list parents have provided in advance or to someone with a written request form. Other centers realize that phone call requests are sometimes necessary. One such center has a policy of asking a child released to a person not on the designated list (in response to a phone request), "Do you know this person? What is the person's name?" The policy states that the center will not release a child to an adult whom the child cannot call by name (or by relationship title such as Grandma).

Some day-care centers keep doors locked, and they issue keys to parents so that they may enter the facility without ringing a bell or interrupting the flow of activity within a learning area. If you are given such a key, take care of it. Don't give it to anyone else.

If you see a gap in the security system, speak up. Discuss the subject with the center's director.

Field Trips Ask questions about security measures for taking field trips or even going across the street to the park. Do enough adults accompany the children?

Talk to Your Child Don't rely on a young child to remember at all times what you say to him about security. Do instill in your child the warning not to go anywhere with a stranger. Ask your child to tell you what a stranger is. Make sure your child knows *by name* with whom she has permission to leave the day-care facility.

9 ✳ Group Size and Supervision

A primary way of evaluating a childcare provider is the ratio of adult staff members to children. Also important is the total size of the group. Here is a fairly standard guideline:

Ages	Number of Adults	Maximum Group Size
Newborn to 3 months	1 adult to every 2 children	2
3 months to 2 years	1 adult to every 4 children	4
2 to 3 years	1 adult for every 5 children	10
3 to 4 years	1 adult for every 7 children	14
4 to 5 years	1 adult for every 10 children	20
5 to 6 years	1 adult for every 13 children	26

Learning centers usually strive for slightly lower ratios since specific skill training and even reading may be part of the curriculum.

Individual Attention Within a group setting, your child still needs individual attention. Look for that as you tour a center. Is a teacher occasionally sitting with one child alone, perhaps working on a problem or listening intently to one child tell a story? Does the caregiver seem to have eyes only for the group to the extent that he fails to see the individual child in need?

Small Group Interaction Within a larger group, your child will no doubt be part of a small group cluster. Children who play together or learn together tend to cluster naturally in groups of two to four. Are the teachers trained to assist in this clustering process? What happens to children who are left out of the group?

Segregation by Age You will want to make certain that your child's group is in some way separated from other age groups—in most circumstances. Even in a home-based option, you'll probably want the children to be clustered in the same age range. Segregation by age permits your child to experience the greatest amount of peer interaction and participation in activities that are both appropriate for age and stimulating for particular growth needs. Look for separate playground areas, for example, and separate activity rooms for older and younger children.

10 ★ Age Appropriate- ness

Every child is unique. At the same time, children tend to move through stages of development that are fairly predictable. The stages tend to happen rather fast and furiously during the first five years of a child's life. Therefore, evaluate the extent to which the facility takes into consideration various stages of development and provides toys, equipment, and books accordingly.

Age or Developmental Level? Ask the facility's director how the children are separated into classes or groups. Is it strictly by chronological age? Or is it by abilities (the child's developmental age)? Is the center geared toward children of one grouping more than another? For example, does the school enroll mostly three- and four-year-olds, with very few five-year-olds and virtually no babies or toddlers?

Your child is likely to be in a grouping for an entire year. How does the curriculum or activity schedule reflect the changes that are likely? Look for elements and activities geared toward your child's age level.

Under Two Children of this age have a strong desire to touch. They need lots of hugs and hand-holding. They are eager to touch everything around them and to get a sense of what they are capable of manipulating on their own (through pushing, pulling, probing, prodding, and pounding). Are the toys and materials geared toward child manipulation, with bright colors and stimulating sounds? Are the toys virtually indestructible and safe for child handling? Children of this age need frequent feeding and sleeping times, also. Does the schedule accommodate these needs?

Two to Three This period in a child's life is marked by large muscle development. Children enjoy climbing, jumping, and riding. They love to try new things and have plenty of space. At the same time, they have little sense of danger (related to themselves or others), and they have a fairly low frustration level. Does the facility provide safe and adequate outdoor and indoor play equipment that requires large muscle use?

Two- and three-year-olds have keen powers of observation and are sponges for language-related activities. Does the facility have storytelling times and a circle time for talking? They have short attention spans and need naps and frequent snacks. Does the schedule provide for these needs?

Three to Four   Three- to four-year-olds learn
to play with others and also begin to develop small
muscle coordination. They enjoy manipulating
paintbrushes, drawing or coloring with crayons, fit-
ting pegs into holes, and working puzzles. They
have a rich fantasy world and like to dress up and
pretend with puppets, dolls, and store or house environments. They are beginning to learn letters
and numbers. They are very observant. Does the
center provide materials and activities for enhanc-
ing all of these developmental skills?

Four to Five   This is the age of intense curiosity, game playing, and building. Four- to five-year-
olds enjoy Legos, cooking, arts and crafts, simple
board games, and group games. They usually are
beginning to read or at least are aware that letters
make words and words convey stories; therefore,
they need some alone-time with books that they
can start to read for themselves. They love to learn
songs and do projects. The tendency is to overload
them with pencil-and-paper activities. But four- and
five-year-olds still need lots of physical activity and
a wide variety of stimulation.

Five-Year-Olds   Many day-care and early
learning centers provide kindergarten. Children
are prepared more intentionally for reading and
writing with a pencil. Social skills are emphasized.
The goal is to achieve readiness for school. Specific behavioral objectives, defined activities, and a

highly structured schedule are usually provided. Ask how the school district defines readiness and what the day-care or early learning center does to help a child meet school readiness criteria. A center offering kindergarten needs to have teachers trained and experienced in teaching that grade level.

11 ✦ Cost Factors

The cost of full-time childcare varies widely. All things considered, it takes a fairly substantial family income to pay for private full-time preschool (and especially for more than one child).

Full-time day-care centers can run from $40 to $150 a week, depending upon the city or town. The national average currently hovers around $65 a week.

One company-related center charges $500 per child per month, which sounds high. But the hours of operation are 6:30 A.M. to 8:00 P.M., and the average child spends up to nine hours a day in the center—fifteen minutes before and after the parent's eight-and-a-half-hour shift.

At the other end of the spectrum, consider the parents of three children (under the age of six) who hired an in-home caregiver for $800 a month. That was by far the most cost-effective option for them.

Fee Variations Some day-care centers have sliding fees based on family income. Others offer discounts to families with more than one child enrolled. Still others have scholarships available.

Some preschools and early learning centers give discounts if a parent will volunteer a certain number of hours a week or month.

Ask about payment plans.

Get all of your financial obligations in writing before you enroll your child. For example, how many months do you need to pay at a time? Is there a deposit required? What is the overtime policy and fee?

A Private Sitter   If you are hiring a nanny or private sitter, spell out clearly, and in writing, the person's monthly salary and any benefits you are providing, such as food or a transportation reimbursement. Discuss what you consider to be a fair overtime policy, and anticipate the amount of overtime you may require in a month. You are responsible for Social Security payments on behalf of a private childcare provider.

Tax Credits   Day care qualifies for certain tax credits. Take advantage of any deductions for which you may qualify.

Co-Ops   These day-care and preschool facilities generally operate on a nonprofit basis. Groups of parents pool their resources and create the school or day-care environment, maintain and provide the facilities and equipment, and hire a qualified teacher. The parents generally serve as teacher aides on a rotation schedule.

Hidden Costs Hidden costs might include the cost of uniforms, the cost of additional transportation (to and from the center), or additional costs for sick days (your loss of pay or the expense of a special sick-child caregiver).

12 ✦ Meals and Snacks

Discover early in the decision-making process what meals are provided for your child and what eating schedule is followed. Some centers and private caregivers provide breakfast. Other centers assume that the child has already had breakfast.

What About Lunch? Is a hot lunch provided? What about half-day participants? If your child stays at the center past five in the afternoon, is an evening meal provided? Ask to see a menu schedule for an average week.

What About Snacks? Does the center provide a mid-morning or mid-afternoon snack? What is offered?

Formula Usually, the parent is required to provide formula or baby food.

Nutrition Discuss with the facility director the way in which menus are planned. One center might emphasize whole-grain, natural-food menus with lots of vegetables and fruits and home-baked bread. Another center might offer lots of hot dogs and canned beans. If you are considering a private baby-sitter or other-home caregiver, ask, "Who does the cooking?" and "What's for lunch?"

Eating Area   Does the facility have a specified eating area? Do children eat according to age level, or do they all flock to a central eating area? Is cleanup after a meal part of the learning process? Is food preparation part of a child's activity?

Kitchen Check   If you are considering taking your child to another person's home for day care, take a peek into the kitchen. Is it clean? Are low kitchen cabinets and drawers childproofed? If the person doesn't have a dishwasher, are paper plates and plastic utensils provided? (Day-care centers are required to wash dishes in water heated to 140 degrees.)

13 * Naps and Quiet Time

A nap is an essential part of a child's daily routine, but it's an event many children openly resist. Most licensed centers require that a child who is in a center full-time rest for at least one hour. Some states require that children be provided with cots and linens that are changed after each use.

Ask about the specific naptime procedure in the place you are evaluating. Are mats used? Are they rolled up or stacked? (Stacked mats provide highly unsanitary conditions!)

Will you be asked to provide a blanket solely for your child's use? What about a pillow? Sheets?

Is a specific place designated for naptime? Are children placed at least a foot apart during naptime (either their mats or cots)? Is the sleeping area quiet and well ventilated?

Infants and Toddlers Young children need more naps. Infants are probably asleep most of the day. Toddlers may need a morning nap as well as an afternoon nap.

Quiet Times Even if a child doesn't want to sleep, he should be encouraged to close his eyes and lie still. Older children may be allowed to take a book with them to the mat or cot and use the time for browsing or "reading."

Alone Times Does the facility accommodate a child's need to spend part of a day alone—simply to rest, relax, reflect, and refocus? Day-care centers and preschools are quite good at providing activities, meals, games, stimulating presentations, playgrounds, and so forth. Usually, less attention is paid to a child's need to be alone or quiet, whether to read, rest, play her own fantasy games or create her own fantasy world, or simply watch the world around her. Is there sufficient space in the center, or on the playground, for a child to isolate himself from others and curl up for a moment or two for alone time? Some centers provide a couple of large beanbag chairs for this purpose. Some have secret gardens or caves (aspects of play equipment or rooms) to which children can retreat.

14 ✦ Discipline and Punishment

Understand clearly—and have *in writing*—an agreement with your childcare provider regarding the extent to which the caregiver can mete out discipline, in what forms, and to what extent.

Face the fact that your child is going to misbehave from time to time. Here are several questions you need to answer:

- What are the caregiver's ideas about what warrants discipline or punishment? (What rules must be followed at all times? What behavior warrants intervention?)
- Do you want the caregiver to require immediate, total obedience?
- What do you want the caregiver to do when children fight between themselves?
- How do you want the caregiver to handle repeated and willful behavioral problems?
- Do you expect the caregiver to accommodate accidents? Do you want your child to be allowed to have accidents, as opposed to willful acts of rebellion or disobedience?

If you and the childcare provider seriously disagree over these very basic discipline issues, find another provider.

At the same time, recognize that no two people are going to be in total agreement on discipline issues because no two people see every situation exactly alike. There's likely to be some difference in the rules established for home, school, and day-care center, but as much as possible, work to keep the differences few and minor.

Corporal Punishment Regulated home care and licensed day-care centers are not allowed to use corporal punishment. Let the day-care provider know what has worked best for your child apart from spanking:

- Verbal chastening
- Having time-outs (isolation from other children)
- Making restitution (cleaning up damage, apologizing)
- Removing certain privileges

An Educational Experience Good discipline teaches a child what to do. A child needs to be told in advance what behaviors are acceptable and desirable and what behaviors are not allowed and the consequences for misbehavior. Punishment, then, becomes corrective—moving a child

away from undesirable behavior and toward desired behavior.

Punishment vs Embarrassment Your
child should be punished for wrongdoing without
embarrassment. Never should your child be made
an example for other children. Discipline should
be direct, personal, and private.

Consistency and Immediacy The most ef-
fective discipline is consistently and immediately
enforced. If something is wrong on Monday, it
should be wrong on Tuesday. You will want your
day-care provider to discipline your child in a
timely fashion. Delayed punishment is not effec-
tive with young children.

Beware of "the Gap" Children who have
behaved all day long in a day-care environment
sometimes become unruly as soon as their parents
arrive on the scene. It's as if children uncon-
sciously sense that the period in which parents and
caregivers are both present represents a discipline
gap. Assume that from the moment you are in your
child's presence, you are in charge of discipline
and punishment.

15 ✻ Abuse: Defined and Recognized

Perhaps parents' worst nightmare is that their child will be abused by a person to whom they have entrusted the child for care. In fact, less than 2 percent of reported child abuse cases involve day-care providers. Nonetheless, parents should acquaint themselves with what constitutes abuse and how to recognize it.

Physical Abuse Physical abuse may be as basic as pushing, pinching, or pulling hair, or as serious as battering that results in bruises, broken bones, or internal injuries. Any action that causes willful physical harm or pain to your child should be considered abusive.

Sexual Abuse Your child's day-care environment must be free of sexual innuendo or sexually oriented jokes. It should be free of sexually explicit books, magazines, music, or videos (especially important in considering other-home day care or in hiring baby-sitters). The day-care provider must never touch your child in a way intended to arouse your child (or the adult) sexually, expose either the child's or the adult's genitals, or attempt any form of sexual intercourse, oral copulation, or sodomy.

Emotional Abuse This form of abuse includes threats, teasing, demoralizing comments, fear-causing suggestions, forcing a child to do what he doesn't want to do, humiliating a child in front of others, or in any way punishing a child so that the punishment interferes with the child's eating, sleeping, or elimination.

Neglect Neglect can vary from not responding to a child's cries to not properly storing chemicals to not watching a child closely while she is in or near a swimming pool. Anything that creates a situation in which a child may cause herself harm can be considered neglect and, thus, abusive.

Signs of Abuse The Crime Prevention Center of the Office of the Attorney General has published these following signs of abuse:

1. Stained or bloody clothing.

2. Major changes in school performance and sleeping patterns, including the onset of nightmares or a sudden fear of falling asleep.

3. Compulsive masturbation or unusually seductive behavior with classmates, teachers, and other adults.

4. Age-inappropriate behavior such as bed-wetting or thumb sucking.

5. Sudden acquisition of money, clothes, or

gifts with no reasonable explanation. Some pedophiles will shower their young victims with presents as one way of enticement.

6. Physical injury or irritations to the genital area, such as pain, itching, swelling, bruising, bleeding, cuts, or scrapes.

7. Halting attempts to tell a friend or trusted adult such things as "I know someone" or "What would you do if . . ."

If you see any of these signs, confront the day-care provider immediately. Also look for these behaviors in your child:

- Frequent telling of stories about bad things that supposedly happen to other children or to someone your child won't identify by name.
- Exhibiting fear at going to the day-care center or exhibiting heightened fear in response to the presence of a particular person.
- Desiring suddenly to stop an activity the child has been enjoying.

16 ✦ Abuse: Prevented and Confronted

You must take steps to prevent abuse, but if you think it has occurred, confront it swiftly and decisively.

Prevention The first way to prevent abuse is to train your child at home in such a way that

- he knows what is acceptable and what is inappropriate behavior. Let him know that his body is his own. Teach your child which parts of his body are private and should not be touched by another person.
- she has the confidence to say no to an adult who attempts to act toward her in a sexually inappropriate way.

Second, make unannounced visits to your child's day-care center. Stop in as you run a business errand or as part of an early lunch break. Do you find the caregiver always harried, angry, or highly frustrated? What is the tone of voice used when talking to, or about, your child?

Suspecting Abuse   If you suspect abuse, talk to other parents of children who are part of the program or under the baby-sitter's care. Is there a general pattern you can detect? You won't want to spread malicious gossip or encourage a witch-hunt, but you do want to let other parents know of your concern and ask for their advice and input.

Also talk to the caregiver in a nonthreatening, nonaccusatory way about the problem or changes in behavior that you are seeing in your child. Ask if the person has noticed changes in your child's behavior. Ask if there has been a change in the routine at the center. Ask if any new employees have been hired. If you see bruises or scrapes or blood on your child's clothing, ask what happened.

And then, watch closely to see the caregiver's reactions. Is she willing to discuss the matter, or does she discount the situation as unimportant? Is she hesitant to reply? Does she become defensive? Does the answer sound very glib?

Confronting Abuse   If evidence such as unexplained bruises or blood-stained undergarments points toward an abusive situation, talk to the daycare center supervisor as soon as you can. Go with other parents if others have similar situations or concerns. And withdraw your child from the center until action is taken or the situation is resolved to your satisfaction. If you are dealing with a private individual, it's better to err on the side of dismissing the individual.

17 ✳ Abuse: Reporting and Recovery

Reporting Abuse   You may want to seek out an ally in a teacher, doctor, or day-care director. These professionals are required by a mandatory reporting law (in all fifty states) to file a report if abuse is suspected.

Your goal in reporting abuse is to protect your child from further abuse and to make sure that the offender has no opportunity to hurt another child. Sometimes the two goals are in conflict. For example, parents may view the legal-reporting procedure as something that would cause further emotional trauma to their child, and they decide not to file charges. Parents need to recognize that their failure to report abuse leaves their child wondering forever if the abuser is "out there" somewhere, waiting to victimize him again.

Some parents don't report abuse because they don't want to make waves or don't want to falsely accuse an innocent person. It's better to file charges and have an innocent person exonerated than to let an abuser go free to hurt another child.

Still other parents don't report certain kinds

of abuse—especially emotional abuse—because they don't think it's as harmful as physical or sexual abuse. That isn't so. Children can bear the inner wounds of emotional abuse their entire lives.

Help for the Abused Child First and foremost, let your child know that you believe her, that you will do everything in your power to help her and protect her, and that you are sorry beyond words for what has happened.

Second, be open to talking to your child about the experience and listening to your child's response. Don't shut the door on the incident and hope that it will disappear. It won't. Children need to talk about what has happened to them—sometimes repeatedly through the years as they reach different stages in their maturation.

Third, contact a person who specializes in abuse recovery, preferably someone who works with children. Recognize that abuse affects the entire family. Provide professional counseling for your child as long as he needs it.

Fourth, assure your child that she is not responsible for what has happened. The abuser must be given the total responsibility for abusive behavior.

Fifth, don't allow your child to be bullied or teased by those who may have heard about the abuse. Insist that other people treat your child with respect.

18 ✶ Touching and Holding

As much as you don't want your child physically punished or abused, you probably do want your child to know the warmth of a loving caregiver's touch and embrace.

You'll want your child to receive appropriate touching behaviors, especially those linked to

- affection. An arm on the shoulder can say to a child, "I like you."
- praise. A pat on the back or shoulder can send the message, "You did a good job."
- sympathy. A hug or touch on the arm can send the message, "I'm sorry."
- comfort. Picking up a child who has fallen and hurt himself is an appropriate gesture.

Observe the Caregiver in Action Watch to see how children respond to the touch of a caregiver.

- Are they content? Do they snuggle up, or do they seem to pull away, eager to get down?
- Do they stop crying or increase crying?

• Do they run away from being picked up or shy away from being touched?

Even an infant tends to stiffen or pull away at the touch of a person he regards as threatening or unloving. Older children obviously do the same.

General Body Language   Check out the general cues sent from caregiver to children. Does the caregiver smile at children? Give them thumbs-up signs or quiet applause? Does the caregiver respond to the children with animation in face, voice, and gesture? Does the caregiver get down on a level where children can respond with touches of their own? Or is the caregiver stiff with the children? Stern of expression? Seldom reaching out to them with words or with touch?

Off-Limits   Certain behaviors should generally be considered off-limits—including kissing (especially on the lips), touching below the waist (even love pats on a child's behind), or any form of hugs in which a child is not released when the child wants to be let go.

You'll also want to watch for behavior that the caregiver allows herself to receive from children. Does the caregiver allow children to hit her, throw things at her, or gesture angrily at her without reprimand? If so, such a caregiver is likely to allow violence between children without disciplining it. Does the caregiver let children give her spontaneous hugs? If so, it's likely she's giving those hugs herself.

Infants   Infants need lots of gentle caressing and holding. They especially need to be held as they go to sleep and as they are fed. If you are planning to leave your baby in a day-care facility, find one that is adequately staffed so that your child will get lots of personal attention and holding.

19 ✦ Sick-Child Policy

Ask about the day-care facility's policy regarding sick children.

Defining the Sick Child Children are not generally considered sick if they have only a runny nose or are sneezing. Allergic reactions and colds are seldom regarded as sufficient reason to keep a child at home (from the perspective of parents) and, therefore, have become insufficient reasons for turning away a child at a facility. Usually, a child has to have a sore throat, run a temperature, or have other symptoms related to influenza before the child will be isolated or sent home.

Ask the director whether the center has a policy about notifying parents if the center knows that a child has been exposed to a contagious disease (such as measles or chicken pox) or if an "epidemic" of a certain ailment seems to be sweeping through the center.

Is there a standard procedure for notifying you if your child has a sudden severe headache or begins vomiting?

Is there a standard procedure for telling

you at the end of a day if your child seemed to experience a loss of appetite?

Your child's general health and well-being should be one of the foremost concerns of your childcare provider, just as it is one of your foremost concerns.

Isolation Rooms   By law, a day-care center must have a facility for isolating a sick child where he can be watched by an adult until a parent can come for him. This isolation room is usually located next to the office area so the center's director or secretary can keep an eye on the child. The isolation room should have a comfortable cot and a few toys or books, and it should be near a toilet.

Names on File   As part of your child's application to a day-care center, you'll probably need to supply the names of your child's pediatrician and dentist and the hospital of your choice (or the ones that are part of your medical plan). If you change health-care professionals, notify your child's day-care center. Provide names and numbers of specialists who may be seeing your child—for example, if your child has diabetes, epilepsy, or a heart condition.

In case of a serious injury, seizure, or other sudden and traumatic case of ill health, the center will probably need to be able to notify you quickly for permission to transport your child to a hospital. At the hospital, the physicians and nurses there will need your permission to take appropriate medical action. Know details of this policy, sign all necessary emergency-care release forms, and leave phone numbers where you might be reached at all times.

Insurance Some day-care facilities now require proof of health insurance for the children. Others ask parents to sign forms releasing them of liability in case of accident or illness. Still others acquire massive coverage for themselves and pass the costs along to the parents. What course of action is your childcare provider pursuing?

Immunizations Most childcare providers require proof of age-appropriate immunizations prior to a child's beginning a school year with them. If your day-care provider doesn't ask for this proof, ask about the policy regarding immunizations.

20 ✳ Sick-Child Care

If your child is sick, seek alternative care. Don't insist that your child go to a day-care environment if she is ill. She'll only be more miserable. And she'll infect other children. Sick children who infect other children frequently become reinfected by those to whom they have passed on their ailments! The cycle they initiate or in which they participate can continue for months in a day-care environment, meaning a virtual nonstop series of bouts with the flu, diarrhea, or colds for a child.

At Home Stay at home with your child if you can. He may remember very little else about his years in day care—either positive or negative—but one thing he is likely to remember is this: Mom or Dad was there when I was ill.

If you cannot stay home with your child, try to find someone who can come into your home to provide sick-child care in your absence—perhaps a baby-sitter, a relative, or an adult friend. A child who is ill finds comfort in staying in her own bed and room, surrounded by familiar things and people.

A Service Another option is a service that specializes in sick-child care. A number of hospitals provide this service on a day-by-day or hourly rate. Nurses and nursing aides provide the care and administer medications or treatments, and volunteers usually are on hand to read stories and caress feverish brows.

Some large day-care facilities or day camps have staff nurses and infirmaries for sick children.

Plan B As you make your childcare decisions, come up with a sick-child plan in advance of your child's first illness.

21 ✳ The Smell Test

A quick turnoff to a day-care center or a baby-sitter's home is a foul odor.

If the place where you are planning to leave your child has an odor of rotting garbage, natural gas (which may indicate a leak), exhaust fumes, urine, feces, very stale cooking odors, or a general musty smell, you can probably conclude that the environment is not going to be conducive to your child's health and well-being, even if the toys are bright and fun and the people seem loving and spontaneous toward children.

The Smell of Clean Above all, a facility should smell clean. That doesn't mean the place should have an overpowering pine-cleanser smell, but it should smell fresh, scrubbed, and well ventilated. If there is an unpleasant odor, ask the director or your tour guide about it. There may be an unusual circumstance unique to the day of your visit. If the person showing you around doesn't smell what you smell, go elsewhere. That's a good sign the person is oblivious to the unhealthful conditions.

The prime testing places, of course, are the

center's kitchen and rest rooms, or the baby-sitter's kitchen and bathroom.

Good Smells   Good smells can also tell a great deal about a place. Many day-care facilities situate their kitchens so that normal meal-preparation and even cookie-baking aromas permeate the entire center, which can create a comforting and home-like environment.

22 ✦ Caregiver Profile: The Director

Although a teacher or caregiver is likely to be the person who spends the most amount of time during the day with your child, the center's director is really going to set the tone of the facility and the standard of quality.

Qualifications You'll want to find a center with a director who is an educator. In addition, of course, the person will have to be astute in business matters, be familiar with legislative matters related to early childhood education and day care, and know how to communicate with people.

Key Questions When you visit the center, meet the director. Ideally, the director should give you a tour of the facility and answer your questions. Here are some key questions to explore with the director (and the director alone):

- To whom is the director responsible? For a public day-care center, get the name of the person responsible for its management. For a chain or franchised day-care facility, find out who issues which directives. For a private or church-related center, ask about the board or staff member to whom the director may be responsible.

- What is the overall financial condition of the center? If the center is losing money or is only marginally breaking even, what measures are being taken to make sure the doors stay open? A center that is struggling financially is likely to cut corners.

- Who is in charge when the director isn't there? Most centers are open from ten to twelve hours a day, fifty-two weeks a year. It's impossible for one person to be on site all the time.

The People or the Program?
Note the interaction between the director, other staff members, and children as you take a tour of the facility with the director. Does the director take an active interest in individuals or only in the "program"?

23 ✳ Caregiver Profile: The Teacher

Even if your child is with a baby-sitter or in a day-care facility not labeled an early learning center, the primary caregiver is a teacher. Your child will be with this person almost as many waking hours a day as he will be with you. And he will be learning every minute he is awake!

One director looked for this mix of traits in teachers: 2 parts teacher, 1 part nurse, and 1 part playmate. That's not a bad blend!

Qualities Specifically, you'll want to have assurance that your child's teacher

- likes children and likes the job. The day-care worker who truly enjoys getting up in the morning to go and be with the children will go the extra mile for children, have long-term job stability, and take personal pride in the development and success of the children.
- is still learning. The worker who thinks she knows it all is not likely to evoke the curiosity of the children in her care. The teacher who is still a student at heart is more apt to

listen to children and to delight in their experiments and exploration of the world around them.

In all, look for a balance of these qualities in day-care workers: educational background; experience; reliability (job stability); enthusiasm; physical health and stamina; warmth and care; imagination and creativity; responsibility; pleasant personal appearance; good judgment; clear communication; and a relaxed, low-key temperament.

Staff Training Ask the director about ongoing or in-service staff training provided to the caregivers. This will give you a feel for the amount of supervision and guidance a caregiver receives from the director. Ask about the staff's involvement in making general center decisions. A caregiver who has no input into the overall program is likely to have little opportunity to vent frustrations or implement new ideas and may quickly burn out.

24 ✦ Caregiver Profiles: Ancillary Workers

In addition to the director and teachers, your child will encounter other people in a day-care environment.

Cook If you have an opportunity to meet the center's cook (or even if you are interviewing a possible in-home provider or baby-sitter), ask a couple of questions:

- "How do you decide what the menus will be?" Listen for the words *nutrition* and *new recipes*. You want your child to have nutritious meals and snacks, but with variety.
- "How did you come to have this job?" Listen for the person to mention "children," as opposed to "needing work," "good pay," or "I'm not skilled to do much else."

A part of the licensing process is usually a procedure for having menus approved by a qualified nutritionist (especially so that meals will meet a percentage of a child's daily nutritional needs).

The matter of quantity of servings is something else. Does the cook allow for seconds to children who are hungry or not satisfied with one serving?

Janitor A janitor is frequently the only male staff member at a day-care facility. Children tend to gravitate toward him to balance the predominantly female influence of most centers. Is the janitor available full-time? Is he a kind person who values children and expresses an interest in them? Is he pleasant to the children?

Bus Driver Some centers use their own vehicles. Others contract with a transportation service company. Still others provide no transportation. What is the policy at the center you are considering? If drivers are hired by the center, discover what factors are checked out before a driver is hired.

25 ✦ Caregiver Profiles: Part-Timers

In addition to regular staff members, day-care facilities frequently have a flow of part-time helpers.

Older Students Some centers hire older students (teens and college students) on a part-time basis for after-normal-hours work, especially the after-school hours of 4:00 to 8:00 P.M. Ask what qualifications are required and what supervision is given to these students.

Parent Helpers Some day-care centers require a certain amount of parental involvement. Find out what jobs are relegated to parents and what type of training is given to them.

Volunteers People from the community are sometimes involved in a program.

Student Teachers, Nurses, and Social Workers A number of centers now have teaching affiliations with colleges, junior colleges, high schools, or vocational-technical programs. Find out if your child is going to be part of a learning practicum or lab course. Such courses can be quite good and provide a constant source of new information and new ideas that keep full-time teachers on their toes. However, your child should always be in the care of at least one person who is an experienced childcare provider.

26 ✳ After-School Care

The atmosphere of many day-care facilities changes dramatically around four o'clock in the afternoon. Prior to that time, centers are usually humming with a fairly regular routine.

The 4:00 P.M. to 6:00 P.M. Period From four o'clock to six o'clock is a major transition time in many centers, especially those that are on a ten- or twelve-hour-a-day schedule. Some children leave, which tends to cause those left behind to be either envious or relieved. Other children arrive— those who come to a center only after school—and their presence can be disruptive, comforting, or exciting.

Find out how the center handles these hours if your child is going to be there during that time:

- Will a late afternoon snack be served?
- Does the facility serve dinner to children who must remain at the center until after six o'clock?
- Are the children allowed to play outside?
- Are children encouraged to wash their faces

and hands, comb their hair and, in general, get ready to greet parents with a happy face?

• Are parents encouraged to come in for an unwinding story time?

Tutors and Homework Helpers   Some facilities provide homework helpers, especially for those children who come to the center after school. In many instances, high-school students or college students are employed for this purpose. If your child must go to a day-care facility after school and is there for longer than an hour, see that this time is put to good use. If homework helpers aren't provided, there should at least be a couple of rooms designated as study rooms where students start their homework.

Children coming to a center after school usually need a snack, a rest room, and a few minutes of active exercise to expend pent-up energy. Does the facility have recreational equipment for school-age children to use, such as basketballs and hoops or Ping-Pong tables?

Supervision   How many adults are present in the center after regular hours? Some centers advertise their student-teacher ratio based on an overall average. The during-the-day ratio may be quite acceptable, but the after-school ratio may not be.

27 ✳ The Average Day

Once you have pretty much decided on a center, it's a good idea to visit a couple of times unannounced and at various hours during the day. You'll get a distinct feel for what an average day might be like at the center.

Arrival Time This period is from opening to about 9:00 A.M. Parents are often in a hurry, anxious to get to work. Children often sense that anxiety and may be upset, and they may be sleepy or hungry.

Are children greeted warmly and cordially? Is someone present precisely at the announced opening time? Does the center appear ready and waiting for the children?

The Morning Program Morning programs usually involve organized activities related to education—with special attention given to materials and equipment that promote learning. Attention spans and alertness are usually at a peak during these hours. In many centers, teachers with education degrees are employed only during the morning hours.

The Midday Hours   Midday is a time for putting away learning materials, toileting, washing, eating lunch, taking naps, and engaging in quiet, restful activities, such as a story time. The emphasis is generally on taking care of human needs for nourishment and rest.

The Afternoon   This is usually playtime. When weather permits, children frequently are ushered outdoors. The emphasis is on socialization. A visitor during these hours can expect to see lots of activity and hear lots of noise. This is also the time during which field trips are usually scheduled.

Going Home   From about 4:00 P.M. on, daycare facilities seem to wind down. Watch to see how children leave the facility. Are they hurried out the door, or are they told good-bye with a smile? Is the teacher open to spending a few minutes in conversation with you as a parent? How do teachers respond to tired parents?

28 ✦ The Center: Its Look and Sound

A Multipurpose Facility Some centers share space with other programs, such as social clubs or churches. If another group is using the facility, to what extent does the day-care center have its own areas for storage, and to what extent can the children's work be displayed or partially finished projects be left out for completion?

The Playground Regulations usually require that the facility have at least seventy-five square feet of outside space per child using that space. Many centers have a rotating use of outside space. Is the space well maintained? What is the surface of the playground? (If it's predominantly dirt or asphalt, with very little grass, be concerned. Sand and grass areas are quite acceptable.)

General Appearance Look for light. Are there some windows to provide outside natural light? Is the interior of the center painted in bright, cheerful colors?

Listen for the center's prevailing sound. Is it one of children crying and adults yelling, or of children playing and laughing?

Look for "soft" places: an overstuffed chair or sofa, foam mattresses, or a heap of pillows covered with soft, washable materials.

Look for storage. Is there a place where your child can put her things—her coat and knapsack? Is the teacher's space (or closet) orderly and clean?

The Home Facility   These same factors apply to another person's home. Is the outdoor play area (perhaps the backyard) well maintained? Is there enough light? Is there a child-only room for play or learning activities?

29 ✳ The Center: Your Child's Space

A day-care center's space for school-age children is likely to be a classroom. For infants and toddlers, it's likely to be an area that feels more like a nursery. (Licensing regulations require that these two areas be kept separate.)

Toddlers Determine to what extent your child will have an opportunity to move about freely. Toddlers love to roam. You won't want your toddler confined to a stroller or any type of walker.

School-Age Children Even within a classroom, school-age children need to have a personalized designated space to call their own. It may be a chair, a desk, a locker, or even an open cubbyhole. They need to have access to a space where they can be by themselves.

Child-Sized Furnishings Chairs and tables should be appropriately sized, as should sinks and toilets. (If child-sized sinks and toilets aren't available, are sturdy step stools provided so children can wash their hands, get a drink of water, or use a toilet when they need to do so without adult assistance?)

Plenty of Room   Licensing regulations require thirty-five square feet per child in indoor space. Most centers have more space than that per child.

Is there a chair for everyone? Is there a place at a table for everyone?

Flexibility and Mobility   Is a child able to move about freely in the space when individual activity is permitted? Or is the room so crowded with furniture and equipment that a child's mobility is impeded? Does the design of the center allow for maximum flexibility—for chairs and tables to be moved easily by groups of children so that open spaces can be created for group activities, games, and performances?

An Inviting Look   Again, look for brightness and cheer in your child's immediate classroom or nursery area. Are the walls decorated with visually stimulating materials or children's work?

30 ✦ Opportunities for Motor Skill Development

During the day-care years, children are rapidly developing their physical skills. To this end, children need an environment that allows them to be physical.

Run, Climb, and Jump Outdoor play equipment needs to be provided that will allow your child to run, climb, and jump as well as push and pull objects (such as on teeter-totters and swings).

Children of this age also love riding tricycles. They enjoy playing with oversized balls and crawling in and out of spaces.

Physical Activities Does the program provide for a round of organized physical activities on a daily basis? Some centers provide dance lessons. Some begin the day with a series of stretching exercises or a period of rhythmic aerobics. Other centers organize group games.

Activities that involve trampolines and tumbling mats need to be closely supervised, of course, but these are very popular and beneficial activities for young children who are eager to try their skills at tumbling. Low balance beams and punching bags are also good physical activity items.

Learning by Doing   Toward the goal of developing large muscle motor skills, a child should have access to such toys and indoor equipment as the following:

- Large blocks
- Sandboxes
- Pounding benches
- Foam balls

Try to get a feel for what percentage of your child's time in the day-care facility will be spent doing things that require physical exertion and what types of activities might be included in an average day.

Physical Activity Rules   What rules govern physical activity? Most centers have rules that prohibit biting, kicking, pinching, hitting, shoving, tripping, and so forth. Are these rules enforced equally and fairly? Are they enforced strictly?

31 ✳ Opportunities for Socialization

Beware of any environment in which children are told to be quiet and refrain from talking to each other for prolonged periods of time! Children need to talk. After all, they are in the process of learning language.

Children also need time to be together without oppressive adult supervision so that they might begin to learn how to organize themselves, supervise themselves, and accomplish tasks together in a cooperative, noncompetitive way. In other words, they need opportunities to learn to play together.

Working Together To children, much of what adults might consider work is actually fun. A number of day-care centers involve children in the work of the center—such as getting out and putting away lunch dishes, silverware, and napkins; scrubbing tables and other hard surfaces; or sweeping porches and floors.

Performing Together Does the center provide opportunities for children to learn to sing together, march or dance together, play instruments together (generally of the toot and tap variety), or perform skits together? Are children encouraged to complete projects together—perhaps painting a mural or building a huge fort that requires all the blocks and lots of architects? Are materials available so that children can dress up and experiment with role-playing? Does the center have puppets children can use in telling stories to one another?

Activity Centers for Social Grouping

Most day-care facilities provide equipment and play sets that allow children to play house, school, store, or workshop. Does the center also have floor puzzles or puzzles that children might work together? Some centers have large floor mats depicting towns so that children might play together in moving toy cars from place to place.

An Open Expression of Feelings

Look for a day-care center in which children are encouraged to laugh openly, to giggle uncontrollably at times, to cry when they are hurt, to express fear, and to vent their anger and frustration in productive, nonharmful ways.

A Spirit of Cooperation

Does the day-care center openly pursue a philosophy of cooperation, or is competition a big part of the center's philosophy? Most parents will want their children in a cooperative atmosphere. There's plenty of time in regular school for children to learn about competition. In a day-care or after-school environment, children seem to benefit more when the atmosphere is that of a family working and playing together.

As you visit a childcare facility, watch to see how the adults encourage active participation from children who seem shy or outside the social group. Are all children treated as equally valuable and worthy of the caregiver's attention? Are all children treated with dignity and respect? Are any children isolated from the group? Does the teacher allow children to shun or speak ill of any child? If so, find another place for your child. These are also things to watch for should you consider leaving your child in the care of a person who is taking care of children in the home, especially if the person's children are included in a larger group.

32 ✦ Opportunities for Intellectual Growth

Your young child is learning continually—whether the education is intentional or not! Your child will learn a great deal in life simply by watching and copying the behavior of the adults around him. If you want your child to have an open-minded, curious outlook on the world, begin to develop analytical skills, and have a growing interest in language, art, and music, choose a caregiver who embodies the same traits.

Blocks, Puzzles, and Building Kits Children develop analytical skills and the foundation for math skills by working puzzles and building things with blocks, play logs, Tinkertoys, Legos, and other types of building sets. They learn memory skills by playing with certain games and puzzles.

Drawing, Painting, and Writing Children should be given an opportunity to manipulate pencils, crayons, and paintbrushes—to prepare them for school activities, to develop their eye-hand coordination, to enhance small muscle development, and to develop their creative and artistic expression.

Numbers and Letters Day-care centers should have materials that encourage the learning of numbers and letters.

Stories and Storytelling A day-care center can stimulate intellectual growth by the frequent reading aloud of books, and by encouraging free-form storytelling. "Show and tell" is a form of storytelling.

A "Library" Does the day-care center have a library? It may be a reading corner with a carpet, a few pillows, and a bookshelf with plenty of picture books.

Science Projects Objects appropriate for a science corner include tools for measuring (from rulers to thermometers to scales), magnets, and a magnifying glass. Some centers set up a fish tank, gerbils' cage, or ant farm.

33 ✱ Testing

Day-care centers test children for various reasons. Sometimes the program is a preschool operated as part of a university course or educational experiment, and tests are a means of measuring the progress of the overall group, or of gaining research data related to a particular aspect of a program. Sometimes tests are conducted to help diagnose what seems to be a persistent or recurring physical or emotional problem in an individual child.

The two main concerns that you should have as a parent are these:

• Will I be notified before any test is given to my child?
• Will I be fully informed as to the test results (and their implications)?

You should always retain the option of deciding that your child not be tested. You also have the right to know all that a test might involve and if there's any possibility of your child missing out on key aspects of the center's program because she is part of a control group that doesn't receive an extra stimulus, experience, or exposure to new information.

Entrance Tests   Some early learning centers and private preschools require testing before a child can be admitted. These centers tend to use the Stanford-Binet or the Wechsler Preschool and Primary Scales (WPPSI) as their means of standard intelligence testing, and they nearly always require an interview with the child.

   However, children rarely do their best in a strange environment or with testers and interviewers they have never seen before. And the tests rarely measure things that are important for a preschool to know about a child. Children develop intellectually in spurts. There's nothing about an IQ test that measures adaptability or potential for growth. IQ tests frequently show great variation in results during the first eight to ten years of a child's life.

   It is very likely that a child can score poorly and have that test score be a complete fluke. That error may haunt a child for the rest of his life—giving him a sense of failure or putting him on an educational track that will keep him from reaching his potential. Spare your child this trauma!

Kindergarten Readiness   One of the tests most widely used by schools to test for kindergarten readiness is the Gesell School Readiness Test. This test isn't always a good measuring device. A trained person must administer it and interpret it, and even so, some research has shown that as high as 50 percent of those tested are misdiagnosed. The best judges about whether your child is ready for kindergarten are you and your child's immediate caregiver or preschool teacher. Talk over your child's progress. Ask specifically along the way:

- Is my child motivated to learn and to learn more?
- Does my child ask pertinent and insightful questions?
- Is my child capable of receiving instructions and acting on them?
- Does my child have an ability to concentrate on a task and to stick with it until its completion?
- Is my child on a steady growth track—both intellectually and emotionally?

34 ✦ Evaluations and Consultations

Not all day-care centers provide written reports regarding the progress of a child. Certainly, such reports aren't a must.

As a parent, you'll want to know

- when problems arise. You'll want to know if your child is having a particular difficulty emotionally, physically, or intellectually. Ask the teacher periodically, "How is my child doing?" or "Is my child having any problems that I might help remedy?" or "Does my child seem to have difficulty learning any aspect of the material you are presenting?" An expression of genuine interest nearly always gets an honest, straightforward response.

- your child's successes. No parent wants to hear only when a child misbehaves, fails, or is going through a tough period of adjustment. Look for a day-care provider who not only will tell you about your child's successes but will let you share in some of those moments. Know whenever a performance is scheduled. Even if you can't attend, you can ask your child details about the performance, his role, and how he felt after the performance was over.

One day-care center provides work folders for parents to peruse at their leisure. The folders are made available to parents in a centralized area where they can look at them without their children present if they so desire. Teachers put student drawings, paintings, scribbles, and other items into the folder. Items are dated and removed after a month so that the folders don't grow too thick. Parents are allowed to take home any of the items they want to keep. Such a system provides an ongoing means of evaluation that can be very beneficial to a parent.

Conferences with the Caregiver Have a formalized encounter with your child's caregiver at least twice a year. This also goes for those who opt for more informal care—such as a neighborhood baby-sitter or in-home care.

- Meet privately with the caregiver. And make certain that all information you exchange is confidential. If at all possible, both parents should be present. (If a housekeeper or grandparent is a significant part of a child's life and daily schedule, that person might be invited to come along.)
- Have an open-ended agenda. All matters of importance should be considered—from tan-

trums to food preferences to learning achievements.

- Express any home-related behaviors or changes in circumstance that you feel might affect your child's success at the day-care center. For example, if a member of your family is undergoing treatment for a serious ailment, the day-care provider should be told.

- Ask for suggestions from the caregiver. Ask, "What more might I do to help my child?" Every parent can benefit from pointers offered by an objective, caring person.

You'll probably want to compare your child's current level of performance and skill to the last time you had a conference. The program should have some type of continuity in record keeping.

Listen carefully to what the caregiver says. Be especially sensitive to times when you suspect that the caregiver is choosing words with extra caution. Is there a problem the person doesn't know how to express?

Avoid blaming the caregiver. If your child is having a problem, focus on how you and the caregiver might forge a solution.

If you aren't able to cover everything you want to talk about in the time allotted for your conference, schedule a follow-up appointment.

General Reports   Pay attention to any and all papers that your child brings home. They can vary from menus to progress reports to field trip announcements to a successful writing of numbers one to ten. In looking at what comes home from the day-care center or preschool on a regular daily basis, you'll have a good feel for what is happening at the school and how your child is doing.

Be wary of the center that issues grade reports or highly formalized and detailed analyses of your child's progress. More time may be spent analyzing your child than teaching your child or guiding her socialization.

35 ✦ Field Trips

Young children love to take field trips and explore the big world outside their homes and day-care centers. Downtown day-care centers frequently take walking tours of their area. Centers located near parks sometimes make park visits a part of the weekly routine.

Details In talking with the center's director, ask about field trips:

- "Where do you go on field trips?"
- "How often do you take them?"
- "Is there an extra fee?"
- "Do all of the children participate or only those who can afford to go?"
- "How are children transported?"
- "How many adults go on a field trip?"
- "Are parents always notified about field trips in advance?"
- "Does the center have insurance to cover any accidents or mishaps?" (Are you expected to provide that coverage?)
- "Do opportunities exist for parents to go

along on field trips?" If so, this is something you may want to schedule periodically.

Neighborhood Caregivers An in-home caregiver may plan to take your child along on errands. How often will your child be leaving the home of the caregiver? How adequate is the caregiver's transportation? Discuss how these outings might affect your child's regular schedule, especially eating and sleeping times. Talk over how you feel your child might benefit from such an outing.

Nannies and Baby-Sitters From time to time, you may want your nanny or baby-sitter to take your child to a special event, go on a personalized field trip to a museum, a gallery, or the zoo, or make an excursion to the closest park. Discuss the outing thoroughly, especially issues related to security and transportation.

36 ✦ Diversity Issues

Most parents want their children to be involved in a day-care or preschool program that includes children from other cultural, racial, and socioeconomic backgrounds. Some neighborhoods, of course, are more likely than others to have a culturally, racially, and socioeconomically diverse profile. The day-care program you choose may have socioeconomic diversity but very little cultural or racial diversity. Or the children may reflect racial and cultural diversity but be primarily from the same socioeconomic level.

Diversity provides a richness of experience for your child. He will encounter customs, vocabulary, and ways of acting, working, and expressing that he has never encountered before. Ask the day-care center director about the diversity of the children and what activities are included in the program for children to explore and discuss their diversity.

Parental Involvement If you are concerned about your child being one of a minority in the day-care environment, periodically visit the center to provide input appropriate to your culture. Ask the

director if you might read stories to the children—
perhaps even stories that reflect your culture. Volunteer to go along on field trips so that the children can get to know you as a person. Encourage
your child to take along show-and-tell items that
reflect certain aspects of your culture.

Boys and Girls Most day-care centers strive
to provide a nonsexist environment. Generally
speaking, you'll want your child to have free access
to all activity areas and all activities.

Commonality in Morality Diversity can
also have a downside to it. As much as parents
might want cultural diversity, they rarely want a
diversity of moral and ethical values in the day-care
or preschool environment.

Ask the day-care provider, "What are the
moral and ethical values that you consider to be
most important? How much variance in values do
you allow? How uniform do you ask children to be
in their behavior? How much do you monitor, and
seek to change, a child's vocabulary [especially a
vocabulary spiced with words you'd rather your
child not know]?"

37 ✶ The Use of Media

Be wary of the day-care center that has a television blaring in the background (including the home of a potential baby-sitter or neighborhood caregiver).

Many day-care centers have been invaded by VCRs. Videocassette viewing is a passive activity. Day-care centers should be places of active participation and active learning. Children should be doing, not viewing.

Computers Be equally wary of a bank of computers in a preschool environment. Computers can be used as educational tools, but they are nearly always more appropriate for older children. In young children, pediatricians have noted eye strain and even eye damage through too much involvement with computer screens. Also note the quality of most computer programs geared toward preschoolers. They are rarely more than rote drills. The skills taught can actually be learned more effectively and more efficiently in other ways.

Music Day-care centers frequently use music as part of the program—as a means of teaching songs or dances to children, as a means of calming children, and as a means of creating an atmosphere conducive to naptime. What type of music is used? What are the criteria for choosing music?

Ask the Purpose If you spot computers or television sets as you tour a center, ask how and how often these pieces of equipment are used. Why are the machines there? You may discover that they exist because fellow parents insisted that they be made available or because the center's board of directors thought they were a good idea in training students for the next century. In nearly all cases, preschool children learn better through active, imaginative, self-initiated play and guided group experiences.

38 ✦ A Welcome Mat for Parents

As you tour a potential day-care facility, be on the lookout for other parents.

If you spot one, stop to talk to him or her for a minute or two. Ask about the parent's involvement with the center. You might ask if you can call later to discuss the center in more detail.

If you don't see any parents, ask the director about parental involvement. Is it desired? Is it considered an interference? Is it limited? Do appointments need to be made, or is a drop-in visit acceptable?

Lunch with Mom and Dad Some day-care centers, especially those located within companies or in high-density corporate areas, suggest that parents have lunch with their children. Some offer adult portions of the same food served the children; others suggest that parents bring their lunches and stop in whenever they like. Take advantage of such programs! They offer an opportunity for your child to feel your involvement and concern in a very tangible way.

Visitors There may be particular people that you don't want your child exposed to, and you certainly don't want your child to feel as if her day-care center is Grand Central Station. May anyone visit? How are visitors regulated or monitored? Who decides whether a certain person should be barred from visitation?

If you have a specific request that your child not be allowed to visit with a certain person, will that request be honored? How will it be enforced?

Sign-In Registry Nearly every licensed day-care center has a registry in which parents sign children in and out. The names of all persons authorized to visit or pick up your child should be on file with the center. Just having a name on file, of course, doesn't mean much unless there's a system of monitoring who takes a child in and out.

Ask the director to explain fully the procedures to ensure that your child go home with you and only you (or your designated representative) and that your child be kept from visitations from people who are not authorized to visit him.

39 ✳ Parent Groups

How active are parents in the operation of the childcare environment you are considering?

Research in recent years has shown repeatedly that the foremost factor determining the quality of schools (at all levels) is parental involvement. When parents, as a group, take an active interest and are involved, children enjoy greater success, have lower absentee rates, and are more motivated to learn.

Co-Ops Some programs are cooperatives—parents sharing the responsibility for hiring teachers and an administrator, and providing facilities and equipment. The neighborhood sitter might also be viewed as something of a cooperative—a group of people in the neighborhood hiring one neighbor to care for their children. In both cases, parents need periodic involvement with other parents. Parental feedback is likely the sole means of determining if the caregiver is doing a good job.

Parents as Aides A number of day-care centers invite—and some even require—parents to work a designated number of hours per week or per month as teacher aides. Head Start is a program in which parental involvement has always been a given.

Volunteer Involvement Parental involvement can be registered in terms of volunteering for field-trip duty, attending parent-caregiver conferences, attending parent meetings, or helping with the day-care center's fund-raising projects. Ask the director,

- "Is there a parents' group?" Periodic programs or meetings are scheduled; they are usually devoted to explanations of new program features, updates on information previously discussed, tours of remodeled facilities, or introduction of new teachers and staff members.
- "Are parents represented on the center's governing board?" Such a policy ensures that parents have input into the center's program and policies, including the allocation of funds.

40 ✦ Child Readiness for Preschool

Your child's readiness to enter a preschool is something that you as a parent are best suited to determine. Usually, a child is ready for preschool about the age of three. Prior to that time, day care for toddlers is the best alternative.

Is your three-year-old child miserable day after day after day of preschool? He probably isn't ready to go to preschool on a regular basis. On the other hand, some children seem to beg for stimulation and social encounters even before they reach the age of three. So, watch your child. Put him first in your decisions about preschool. He'll send signals that he's ready for more stimulation.

Alternatives Not all children should go to preschool. If your child lacks discipline or is having problems, or if your child is extremely dependent on you, preschool isn't the place for her. If your child has plenty of opportunities to play and to socialize with other children, if you habitually expose your child to books, art materials, and a variety of educational toys, if your child is growing in self-reliance, self-identity, and an ability to communicate, and if your child is closely acquainted with warm, caring adults outside the family, she'll probably gain little from a preschool experience.

Phase-In Programs   Many children benefit by going to preschool two mornings a week, then progressing to four or five mornings a week, and finally working their way up to five full days (in many places, classified as six hours) by the time they reach developmental kindergarten or kindergarten around age five.

Other preschools have a phase-in policy that extends over a week or two. The child begins by staying at the center one to two hours, usually with Mom or Dad present. Gradually, the child stays a little longer. Soon, he's staying through lunch on his own, without a parent, next through naptime, and then all day.

Not all parents can take advantage of the luxury of phase-in programs, however. Many parents have a need to place their children in full-time day-care facilities or early learning centers from the time they are six weeks to twelve weeks old. Parents need to be encouraged that, given the choice of a quality program, these day-care experiences can be very beneficial to children.

Two-Stage Programs   Perhaps the best thing you can do for a young child is to find a quality program that provides both day care and preschool. Day care is mostly play, some structured and some unstructured. Preschool includes specific curriculum to develop identifiable intellectual and motor skills. The advantage of a two-stage program is that a parent and a teacher can confer together about the best time to transfer a child to the more curriculum-oriented environment.

41 ✦ Separation Anxiety

Expressions of separation anxiety have little to do with what type of parent you have been prior to taking your child to day care or preschool. Some parents assume that if their children make an easy transition, they don't mean very much to their children. Other parents assume that if their children seem utterly distraught at being separated, they haven't prepared their children well. Reactions are extremely difficult to predict. Good parents prepare their children to meet other people, encounter new circumstances, and find their way in a new place. At the same time, good parents realize that their children have wills, desires, and personalities of their own—they sometimes behave the way they want to behave, regardless of prior training.

Empty Nest Blues Parents experience separation anxiety—a feeling of sadness and nostalgia, as if a stage of life is over. If your child senses that you aren't handling very well her going to preschool, chances are that she won't handle the idea very well, either.

Transition Time   You may help the transition from home to day care or preschool in several ways:

- Tour the day-care facility with your child.
- Talk about going to preschool with your child for several weeks in advance of his actually going.
- Ask if a phase-in program is available.
- Assure your child that you will return for her.
- If your child is more comfortable going to the center or school with a blanket, favorite toy, or stuffed animal, let him take it along.
- Try to enroll your child at the beginning of a term if at all possible.
- If your child has just experienced a major illness or the family has been going through a crisis, delay your child's start of day care or preschool awhile if you possibly can.
- Recognize that separation gets better and easier with time.
- Look for guidance from the day-care staff or preschool teachers.
- Don't punish your child for clinging behaviors.

42 ✦ Blending Your Home and the Day-Care Center

A crossover between home and school should definitely be established. You can achieve this in several ways.

Develop a home library   Your child will encounter books at the day-care center or preschool. Let him explore books at home, too. Visit your local community library together, even when your child is still a toddler. Let him attend story hours and pick out picture books. Take him to the bookstore occasionally to buy books. He'll begin to be more comfortable in all environments where he encounters books.

Have some of the same school toys and puzzles at home   Rotate your child's toys and puzzles so that there always seems to be something new in the toy box. At a certain age, your child will recognize that the new toy is actually an old familiar friend. That's all right, too. Children find comfort in the familiar. Having the same or similar toys at home provides a bridge of familiarity for your child and allows her to develop certain skills at home that she can transfer to school. That can be important for your child's self-esteem and confidence among her peers.

Go with your child to a park, and let him play on the outdoor equipment   Give your child an awareness that the day-care center is a place for fun, but it's not the only place.

Let your child take some familiar objects from home with her to school   It may be a toy, blanket, pillow, doll, or stuffed animal. As your child begins to participate in show-and-tell times, the variety can increase. By taking things to school from home and bringing home papers and projects from school, your child begins to see more and more connections between the two worlds.

Keep the same preschool or day-care center schedule in your home on weekend days   Follow the same general day-care routine with your child on Saturdays and Sundays—stimulating activities and events in the morning, free-form play in the afternoon. Eat meals and take naps at the same time. Your child will find it easier to adjust to the Monday-to-Friday schedule of the day-care center.

43 ✳ Toileting Issues

Toileting is a major concern for day-care centers and preschools. Most preschools won't enroll a child who is still in diapers. The reason is a very practical one: centers must have two separate facilities if some of their children are still in diapers; different health codes also apply. Plus, it's a lot easier to conduct a program if toileting is a do-it-yourself activity.

Don't force toilet training in order to enroll your child in a preschool. That extra pressure is likely to backfire, and all of your hard work may go into reverse once your child is actually at school. In fact, toilet training frequently seems to regress when children enter day care or preschool. Separation anxiety often displays itself in accidents.

Children are usually toileted several times during a morning session in a preschool, and teachers are adept at looking out for the child who always seems to wait too long or the one who needs some help. Teachers are trained to help children learn how to use regular toilet seats (as opposed to potty chairs) and how to be hygienic.

Have a frank discussion with your child's primary caregiver at the time your child enters day care or preschool. If your child is just out of diapers, say so. If she's fully trained but still uses a potty chair, say so. Always let the school know if your child is having a chronic elimination problem.

Diapers and Related Supplies If your child is still in diapers, you may be required to furnish diapers along with any other related supplies. Day-care facilities nearly always require disposable diapers. Some centers bill you for the number of diapers used in a day. As your child grows, of course, these needs change.

Initial Toilet Training If your child is in day care from a very early age, her childcare provider may be the first one to notice signs that your child is ready to start toilet training. Coordinate your efforts. The day-care center usually has a pretty good game plan to follow, and because older children are usually around as role models, the toilet training process usually begins earlier, takes less time, and is less traumatic for the child.

44 ✳ Special-Needs Children

The Council for Exceptional Children considers special-needs children to be those who differ significantly from other children their age. Special-needs children have emotional or physical development patterns that fall outside norms for their age grouping. The reason for these developmental differences may be physical, emotional, or mental. Children with learning disabilities, cerebral palsy, visual or hearing problems, paralysis, or emotional problems may all be classified as those with special needs.

Two factors need to be weighed in evaluating the day care or preschool appropriate for a special-needs child:

1. How wide is the gap between your child's development and the development of other children his age? You may need to reach this decision in consultation with your physician, psychologist, and the childcare personnel at the center or school.

2. Is there a day-care center or preschool in your area that specializes in your child's area of need? If so, you'll probably want to check that first. If you would prefer to mainstream your child,

you'll need to determine how capable a day-care center or preschool is in handling your child's needs.

Mainstreaming Questions It's not enough that you think mainstreaming is a good idea or that the childcare provider agrees to take your child. You need to determine precisely what advantages the center holds for your child. Spend an entire day at the center and try to imagine your child in each setting and situation. Then, visit the center again with your child. Watch how the teachers interact with your child.

Express all of your concerns to the day-care personnel. Plan to visit the school often to see how your child and the day-care personnel are coping.

Children in Need An increasing number of children are in counseling or are on medication because of chemical imbalances or emotional problems. If your child is taking medication or is in regular psychotherapy for a particular problem, the center or preschool needs to know as much as possible about how the medication works, what side effects are possible, or what problems might occur.

45 ✶ Religious or Moral Education

Some day-care programs are housed in church facilities or are affiliated with churches. That does not necessarily mean, however, that the program has components of religious or moral education built into it. A day-care program may rent Sunday school rooms or synagogue facilities, and the church or synagogue may have no input into the program or no authority over the center's personnel.

Ask a church-associated childcare provider these questions:

- "What type of moral or ethical training is included in your center's program?"
- "Are you using a particular curriculum that advocates certain theological or doctrinal stands?"
- "Do your teachers sign or give assent to a particular doctrinal or theological position?"

You may want to know, for example, if prayer is offered before meals and snacks, if certain religious holidays are celebrated or honored, if teachers are quick to include mention of God in their lessons or conversations with children, or if some type of catechism training is provided by clergy as part of the program.

Baby-Sitters and Nannies   If you are hiring a person to provide childcare, you'll want to have a conversation about beliefs with that person. What values does the caregiver regard as most important for a child to learn? How does the caregiver define *faith?* What importance is placed on faith development in a child? How might the caregiver help your child develop a set of values and a moral code?

A Major Concern   Parents tend to pull their children from childcare situations most dramatically, quickly, and decisively for two main reasons: evidence of abuse, and disagreements over spiritual principles being taught their children. Values education is one area where you need to be absolutely sure you understand the ground rules of a program. Is the day-care center in support of the values and spiritual principles you desire for your child to have? Or does the day-care center have its own spiritual agenda—for example, to convert your child to its doctrinal positions?

   Don't assume that because a day-care center or preschool is associated with your own church (or own denomination), it is the best possible place for your child to receive care. In most cases, you'll want to find the most healthful and edifying environment and program for your child's total well-being. If the day care or preschool supports you in the spiritual training of your child, that's a bonus.

46 ✹ Contracts and Forms to Anticipate

When the time comes to enroll your child in a day-care center or preschool, you'll probably be asked to fill out a fairly extensive form and, in some cases, to sign a contract.

Financial Agreements You will probably need to state how many hours a day, how many days a week, and perhaps how many months in the year you expect your child to be at the facility. Your fees will probably be based upon that number of hours and the age of your child. Fees, including any overtime fee (which may be broken down into fifteen-minute increments), should be agreed to before your child begins the program. In some cases, you'll be asked to sign a contract that includes a default fee for canceling your child's enrollment or that spells out the notice required before you withdraw your child from the center.

Policy Statements The school's policy statement usually lists all that the facility intends to provide (for example, meals), payment-due schedules, a list of holidays, vacation policy (related to payment of fees), requirement of notification for cancellation, sick-child policy, and so forth.

You'll likely be given a set of rules related to what your child may not bring into the school (including foods and snack items) and what behaviors are considered to be punishable (and in what form). Policies related to suspension or expulsion of a child from the program will be detailed.

Suggestions or rules related to clothing and an appropriate dress code will be provided. If the preschool requires uniforms, that information will be given to you.

A Child's Personal Records You'll be asked to describe any health problems, medications, counseling, disabilities, or allergies your child may have. Some centers also ask parents to describe the child's personality and to identify any major fears the child may have (such as fear of dogs or fear of the dark).

If you are leaving an infant, you'll be asked to supply a feeding and nap schedule, probably on a periodic basis. If your child is a toddler or is entering preschool, you'll be asked about toilet training.

Some schools ask for information related to discipline, your child's ability to use craft and art supplies, and your child's favorite games, books, foods, activities, or toys.

If your child is coming to the center only for after-school care, you'll be asked to give the name of his school, name of his teacher, and phone number of the school.

And, of course, you'll be asked for your name and address, place of employment and address (or phone number), and basic information about your family, such as your marital status and names and ages of siblings.

Medical Information   You'll probably be asked to fill out a medical form with your child's medical history, pediatrician's name and phone number, your choice of hospital, and proof of immunization. Some schools require that a child have a physical examination within three months of enrollment in their programs.

Permission Slips   You should be prepared to sign several standard permission forms:

- Permission for emergency medical treatment
- Pickup authorization (a list of all persons with permission to sign for your child's release from the center)
- A photographic release (which allows a center to take photos of your child for advertising, news, or publicity purposes)
- Permission to go on field trips
- Transportation authorization

Insurance   Some day-care centers require proof of health insurance for your child. In other cases, day-care centers give parents a form stating their coverage.

47 ★ Nannies and In-Home Baby-Sitters

In-home care is generally the most expensive childcare option unless, of course, you have a doting grandmother who works for little or nothing! In some cases, however, you'll find this the most cost-effective means of providing care, especially if you have several young children or need help during unusual hours, on weekends, or around the clock. In-home care is especially good for infants and very young children.

Nannies *Nanny* is sometimes a term implying that the caregiver lives with the family. Others use the term to refer to a full-time baby-sitter. The term generally connotes more than baby-sitting, however, to include a certain amount of education for the child. Professional nannies usually have training or degrees in early childhood development.

Where Do You Find In-Home Care?
Good sources are

- older people, especially newly retired teachers or nurses.
- college students, especially those who take

classes at night (or during hours in which you don't need their help), and especially those who are over twenty-one and in preparation for some type of education, nursing, or social work career.

A number of agencies specialize in nanny placement.

Job Descriptions   Develop a complete job description prior to your search for the right person to be your child's caregiver. Are you expecting the person to do light housekeeping and laundry or perhaps assist with meal preparation? If so, be specific about the duties. If you expect the person to have certain qualifications or skills, say so. If you anticipate that your nanny will be asked to travel with you, have flexible hours, or take your child on frequent excursions by herself, spell out the expectations. You'll need to be prepared to put into writing your financial agreement with the person, including information about days off and overtime. Also be prepared to pay Social Security on behalf of this employee.

Interviews   At the time of the interview, supply the person with a written copy of the job description. Also talk over these issues:

- The person's previous experiences with young children. Ask for references.

- The person's short-term and long-term goals. (You don't want to hire someone who is actively seeking employment elsewhere.)
- The person's values and spiritual beliefs.
- Compensation. You may need to negotiate or compromise in this area.
- House rules that you expect to be followed.

Follow up on references before you make a final hiring decision.

Write It Down   When the time comes for you to enter into an agreement with a baby-sitter or nanny, put your agreement in writing. Cover the same types of things that a day-care center or pre-school would cover. You may want to include a trial period as part of your agreement.

Observation and Orientation   Consider the first few days of a baby-sitter's or nanny's employment to be a time of active orientation and observation on your part. In other words, stay at home, watch, listen, and train. This is vital to the point that you should take off work. Watch how the person interacts with your child. Is she a self-starter, or does she wait for you to authorize or initiate each move? Is she able to discipline your child in a way that brings about a positive change of behavior in your child?

Show her how to work certain machines and gadgets around the house and, if she has responsibilities apart from your child's well-being, how to do chores the way you want them done. Above all, observe your child's response to this person. After the second day, your child will probably have a definite opinion about this caregiver! Do his eyes light up when he sees her come in the door? Does she begin to cry?

48 ✦ Coping with Guilt

Even though parents know they need to, or believe they should, enroll their children in a day care or preschool, parents still tend to feel guilty at times about leaving their children.

Here are some encouraging words for those moments when guilt hits hard.

Guilt is something that stay-at-home parents feel, too You aren't alone in wondering if you are doing the right thing for your child. That's a nagging doubt many parents have a good percentage of the time.

Day care or preschool is not the primary cause of trouble with today's youths Studies show that children who come and go from day care, even from very early ages, do not suffer ill effects if these two mediating circumstances are present in their lives:

1. They are coming from and returning to happy homes.
2. The day-care or preschool center in which

they are placed offers a quality program
with a skilled and caring staff.

Problems don't lie with the fact that a child
attends day care or preschool nearly as much as
they do with facts related to the quality of a child's
at-home life or the quality of the childcare program.

Parenting has been a shared job for centuries In
fact, it's only in the last fifty years that the majority
of parents in our nation have been isolated from
other family members. In the past, aunts, grand-
parents, hired help, and older siblings frequently
took over the role of childcare at least part of a
day. Today, parenting is a very isolated activity,
and for the single parent, a very lonely endeavor at
times. Think of the day-care workers to whom you
entrust your child as something of an extended
family. Treat the day-care center director and your
child's immediate caregiver as being akin to your
family members. Indeed, they are sharing the job
of training your child.

Make the most of your time with your child Talk to
your child as you go to and from day care. Ask
about his experiences during the day (even if he's
only eight months old and can't possibly talk
back). Anticipate the day or your arrival back
home. Share a little about your day. Help your
child voice her feelings. Give your child as much of

your time and attention as you can when you are together.

Recognize that no situation lasts forever   Make the most of each moment you have to experience your child's growing-up years, and also recognize that your child will soon be in school and moving on with his life (and that preschool or day care is only accelerating that process a couple of years).

If you feel persistently guilty, consider alternatives. Perhaps there are ways you haven't yet discovered to readjust your schedule and obligations in order to spend more time with your child. Perhaps one parent can work out of a home office, work only half days, or work different shifts to provide more at-home care.

49 ★ Feedback from Your Child

Periodically, talk to your child very intentionally about her day-care experiences. It need not be a formal talk. It might be as you return from an open house or as you return home from picking up your child at the center. Ask,

- "What do you like most about your pre-school (or day-care center)?"
- "What do you think life would be like if you didn't go here every day? Would the days be as much fun, or would life be as interesting?"
- "Is there anything you really don't like about your preschool?"

Drawings and Stories From time to time, ask your child to make a drawing for you of his day-care center or preschool. See who he puts in the picture. Ask him to describe the various parts of the picture for you. Is the teacher angry or smiling? Is the picture a happy or sad one? Ask your child about the emotions you sense from the drawing: "Sunshine Day-Care Center makes you feel happy, doesn't it?"

Compare drawings over time. If you see a

consistent troublesome pattern, talk to your child's caregiver about it.

Ask your child to make up stories for you about what happens at her day care or preschool. Listen closely. Children frequently couch some of their own fears or concerns in stories they tell.

Body Language Does your child have bad dreams about preschool? Is he reluctant to get out of the van to start his day at the center? Has your child started to have stomach pains, headaches, or frequent bouts with nausea? Does your child pack her knapsack on Sunday evening in eager anticipation of Monday morning's preschool session? These are nonverbal signs that can alert you to problems or joys.

If you sense a problem, talk to your child about it. Sometimes children don't know how to articulate their fears or concerns. You may need to ask, "Is there someone at day care that you hope will be absent today? Is there anybody who seems to pick on you all the time? Do you ever have any fears about not being able to do something?" You may want to talk to your child's caregiver to compare notes and see if you are both being given the same signs. If so, take action. Don't assume that your child will grow out of the problem or that the problem is inconsequential.

50 ✴ Year by Year and Child by Child

Make childcare a year-by-year decision. Don't assume that once you have enrolled your child in a particular place, it will be the place you keep her until she enters kindergarten or first grade. Take each year as it comes.

Moving from Level to Level Sometimes day-care facilities seem particularly adept at dealing with one particular age level. That may be due to a great difference in the number of children enrolled in various levels or to the quality of the teachers assigned to a particular level.

Dropping Out There's no rule that says your child must stay in preschool once he's started the program. If your child enjoys preschool as a three-year-old, but you have a change in your personal situation and desire to have your child home during his fourth year, make the switch! If your child seems to pine for the program he senses is missing from his life, you may want to reenroll him for half days.

Continuity Children benefit from a continuity in place, and they appreciate seeing familiar faces. But for the most part, children are accustomed to meeting mostly new people in their lives. Don't feel you must stay with a program or staff that you've come to regard as mediocre simply because your child has made a few friends there. She'll make new friends in a new place.

Leave Happy If you decide to make a change in your child's day care, make it a happy change. You may want to tell the day-care center director why you are leaving if you believe it will be helpful to the director in improving the quality of her program, but leave on good terms with the staff.

Don't burden your child with all that you've discovered is wrong about a place. Don't speak ill of the day-care center or preschool, and especially don't give a negative opinion in your child's presence.

In talking to your child, speak well of your child's previous baby-sitters, caregivers, and teachers. Applaud the good things they taught your child. Your child will thank you in years ahead for instilling in him a positive, think-the-best-of-people attitude, and he will develop and maintain a more positive attitude toward new learning environments, teachers, and experiences.

The only exception, of course, is abuse. In such instances, assure your child that you are transferring her for her safety and well-being, not because of anything she has done. Do tell others why you are leaving if abuse of your child is the core reason.

Child by Child   Don't assume that the same program or schedule is appropriate for all your children. Each child is different. One child may enjoy preschool at age three and do best in a free-form environment. Another may do better starting preschool at age four and may need a more structured environment. Do what's best for each child.

51 ✳ Positive Parent Talk

On a daily basis, let your child know that you are anticipating a positive experience for him at his day-care center or preschool.

"Just think what fun you are going to have today!"

"I wish I could go on that field trip with you. I think it's going to be a great time."

"I've checked the menu, and you'll have a wonderful lunch today."

Encourage your child to put on a smile even as she buttons up her sweater and gets out of the car.

Don't Build Up Too Much Anticipation

Assure your child that you will be back for him when the workday is over and that you are looking forward to your being together again, but don't build up an evening's activities to the point where your child is looking so forward to nightfall that he misses the lessons of the day. Also, don't promise your child too much out of a day at the center or a day with his nanny. Don't say, "This will be the best time you've ever had," or "You're going to

want to do this many more times in the future."
Maybe not.

Support the Caregiver

Don't allow your child to put you in a position of choosing sides between her and a caregiver. Children, even quite young ones, are very skilled manipulators. If she senses you are feeling guilty, she'll play to that guilt. If she senses she can get more from you by downgrading another person, she'll tend to downgrade.

If your child is continually critical or fussy about a particular person, and you sense it is an attempt to get you to think less highly of that person and more highly of your child, assure your child that you love him beyond measure and always will. State that you can also appreciate the cuteness, politeness, personality, clothing, or accomplishments of other children.

Always speak respectfully of your child's caregiver or teacher to your child, and insist that your child does, too.

Stifle the Criticism

Never criticize your child in front of her peers or her day-care teacher. Few things are as hurtful to a child, even one you may think is too young to notice. Don't embarrass your child in front of peers by telling what you think is a cute story or a funny mistake. Your child may see the instance in a very different light!

52 ✦ Prayer

Never discount the value of prayer in making or living with your childcare decision.

Ask for God's guidance as you seek out a good place for your child to receive care, training, and nourishment Ask specifically for an abundance of wisdom as you research various options and weigh what is best for your child. Before you visit day-care centers or talk with day-care center directors, ask God to bring to light any problems or adverse conditions related to the environment, staff, or program about which you should be aware. Ask for a confirmation that the choice you have made is best for your child.

Pray for your child Ask God to show you how to prepare your child for this experience. On a daily basis, ask God to protect your child at the pre-school or day-care center.

Pray for yourself Ask for comfort during times when you are feeling separation anxiety, and counsel in times when you may feel guilt. Ask for an extra dose of sensitivity so that you might detect problems quickly, and for courage to deal with those problems openly and decisively.

Pray for those who care for your child   Ask God to give them patience, physical stamina, creativity, and a renewal of love for children. Ask God to help them to help your child, and to teach your child only good things that will be of both earthly and eternal benefit.

Pray for your child's friends and their parents   Ask God to enrich the family lives of all who are involved in your day-care center or preschool so that each child who attends will live and move in an atmosphere of comfort, peace, security, and love twenty-four hours a day.

Pray with your child   Send your child off to school with a prayer for his safety, health, happiness, and growth. Include your child's baby-sitter, nanny, or caregiver—and your child's good experiences in a preschool or day-care center—in your nighttime prayers of thanksgiving for the day just past. And pray with hope and faith for a bright tomorrow!

About the Author

Jan Dargatz is also author of *52 Simple Ways to Tell Your Child "I Love You"* and *52 Simple Ways to Build Your Child's Self-Esteem and Confidence.* She holds a doctorate in education from the University of Southern California, Los Angeles.